Credit ABCs for Girls

Inspiring Positive Credit Responsibility for Life

by
Karen J. Gurley

*AuthorHouse™
1663 Liberty Drive, Suite 200
Bloomington, IN 47403
www.authorhouse.com
Phone: 1-800-839-8640*

This publication is designed to provide accurate and authoritative information in regard to the subject matter covered. It is sold with the understanding that the writer is not engaged in rendering legal, accounting, or other professional services. If legal advice or other expert assistance is required, the services of a competent professional person should be sought.

First published by AuthorHouse 6/24/2008

ISBN: 978-1-4343-6501-9 (sc)

Library of Congress Control Number: 2008905099

*Printed in the United States of America
Bloomington, Indiana*

This book is printed on acid-free paper.

Do You Know Your Credit ABCs?

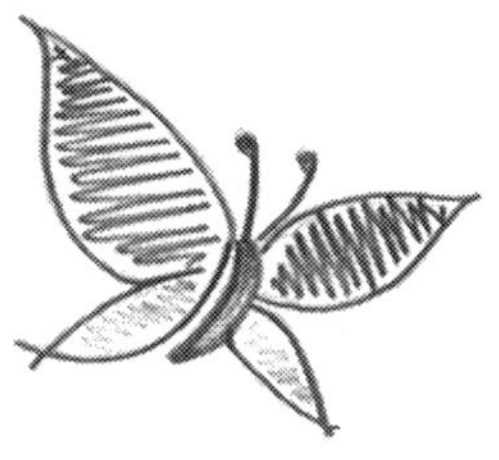

Contents

Acknowledgments

I am very honored to have this opportunity to share such empowering information to so many wonderful teenage girls. Thank you so much to all of you who are interested and take time to read ***Credit ABCs for Girls***.

I'd like to give an overwhelmingly huge "THANK YOU" to Susan Hitchcock, Jasmine Adams, Dorian Denburg, Rachel Niederhoffer and Amira Perryman for making this book come to light through your many hours of editing ... Thank you so much!

Thank you to Ali Hernandez for creating each picture within the book. Your creativity brings these words to life!

On a personal note, I'd like to dedicate this book in loving memory of my parents, Arthur Jr. and Luzean Gurley. In addition, I'd like to thank my incredibly loving and most wonderful mother, Mattie Louise Gurley ... I love you so much!

Thank you to my best friend and lifeline, Marimeko, who is like blood running through my veins. Thank you to my little girl Errin; sisters Cynthia Gurley and Brenda Gurley; and my brother and his wife, Kenneth and Angela Gurley. Also, thank you to my beautiful Aunt Frances and a host of nieces, nephews, cousins, and friends ... I love you all!

Thank you so much Sharon Watts Giles for being my greatest inspiration.

Alice Perkins, my rock, thank you for being an excellent example for practicing positive credit responsibility.

To my Deep Blue family, thank you for providing a fun place for me to express my views and opinions.

Thank you to Roosevelt Giles for believing in me.

A big "Thank You and I Love You" to Amos and Naomi Beasley for your encouragement and strength.

Also, give a big shout out to Salem, my little cocker spaniel.

And last but definitely not least, thank you so much Hailey Gabrielle for letting me know that miracles are very real and that the strongest forces can come in the smallest packages.

Preface

We are a society that encourages the use of credit for every purchasing decision in our lives. However, we do little to teach people how to use credit in a responsible way. This notion is evident in the high number of credit restoration services available throughout our country. In addition, the number of applications for bankruptcy increases each year.

The opportunity to establish credit is afforded to everyone once they turn 18 years of age. This age requirement is lowered if a student is enrolled in college before his or her eighteenth birthday. This means that each year there is a fresh new group of potential customers for those merchants who offer services to allow people to establish credit for the first time.

Consider these facts:

- Graduating high school seniors averaged a failing grade of 52 percent on basic personal finance knowledge in a 2006 national study conducted by the Jump$tart Foundation. *www.jump$tart.com*

- According to a 2005 survey of parents of high school students, 70 percent of parents said their child had not had any formal training in money management, either in school or outside the home. *Visa, Building Teen Personal Finance Skills a Top Worry for Parents, Visa Survey Finds, July 2005*

- Forty-nine percent of teens are eager to learn more about money management, but only 14 percent have taken a class on the topic. *Capital One, Capital One's Annual Back to School Survey Finds Teens Eager to Learn about Money, But Parents Continue to Overlook Important Learning Opportunities, June 2006*

- The Dreyfus Gender Investment Comparison Survey found that parents begin to encourage earning at a younger age for boys than girls (13 versus 16-18, respectively) and are twice as likely to teach boys to save their money. *Tips to Help Younger Women Manage Cash — GreenBayPressGazette.com*

- Sixty-three percent of college undergraduates acquired their first credit card before age 19, and 87 percent of them were freshmen. Seventy-nine percent of college undergraduates have one credit card, and 40 percent of them have a card in their name. *Student Monitor Lifestyle & Media Spring 2006 Financial Services Study, March 2006*

- A 2007 survey by Sallie Mae found that more than half of college students accumulated more than $5,000 in credit card debt while in school. *Sallie Mae, Sallie Mae launches new "Be Debt Smart" campaign to educate students, parents and graduates on managing debt and understanding credit, January 2007*

- According to the 2007 Census Bureau's American Community Survey, in 2006, women made up 56 percent of undergraduates, up from 54.8 percent in 2000. Men made up 44 percent, down from 45 percent in 2000. *Women Feed the Jump in College Enrollment – USATODAY.com, September 2007*
- According to the 2007 Census Bureau's American Community Survey, for every four men enrolled in graduate school in 2006, there were nearly six women. *Women Feed the Jump in College Enrollment – USATODAY.com, September 2007*
- According to the U.S. Department of Education, in 2006, women earned an estimated 58.5 percent of bachelor's degrees, up from 57.2 percent in 2000. Also, women are expected to earn 60 percent of bachelor's degrees by 2012. *Women Feed the Jump in College Enrollment – USATODAY.com, September 2007*

These facts tell us that high school graduates are uninformed about how to manage personal finances and that they do not get any formal training; however, high school graduates want to learn about money management. In addition, parents invest more time in teaching boys about money, while more girls are enrolling and graduating from college.

I coupled these facts with a few more assumptions of my own, such as that females are more emotional spenders, that young ladies are more likely to share their personal information or credit card with friends and family members in order to help in time of perceived crisis, and that young ladies often charge their credit to the limit or over the limit. I immediately came to the conclusion that young ladies are high risk for practicing poor credit responsibility and living a life of less than optimal financial success ... a road that leads to financial burden, depression, and low self-esteem. I concluded this because ladies are most likely to make consistent incomes due to educational statistics and practice poor credit responsibility because they do not receive adequate training on credit responsibility before being given the opportunity to establish credit.

As a result, I believe there is great opportunity to improve the debt crisis that exists in this country today by addressing a large high-risk group one generation at a time. *Credit ABCs for Girls* is an approach to attack this crisis at the root cause by educating the future users of credit on how to practice positive credit responsibility before actually using credit. The results are expected to be empowering. As a successful student of this approach, you will be able to teach others the lessons you learn.

You will learn not to make the same common mistakes so many young adults often make such as:

- Paying bills late
- Charging purchases beyond your credit card limit
- Lending a friend your credit card
- Lending a friend your credit information

This is behavior that can make or break your financial future.

Chapter 1

Credit ABCs
Why Is Credit Responsibility So Important?

"The decisions you make dictate the life you live."

Isn't it wonderful being a teenage girl! If you're not excited, you should be! You're growing up and asserting your independence ... hanging out with your friends, going to parties, driving cars, and managing those special relationships. In addition to all of these fun things, you're also learning how to manage your money. Whether from an allowance or a part-time job, you are spending money that you've earned.

Do you realize that teenage girls and women get a tremendous amount of attention from companies who sell products and services? That's right, companies want something from us. Can you guess what it is? It's our money! Yes, companies are constantly creating things to sell to teenage girls and women and then, after creating them, spending a lot of time and money advertising to us so that we will buy their products and services. Women are their favorite audience because we have more money and can afford to make more purchasing decisions. Think about it: Advertisers often tell us about so many shoes for sale, magazines inform us of the newest fashion trends, we hear about all the hair products and makeup to make us pretty, and so on. Why do you think this is?

Well, I believe the business community discovered one little flaw that teenage girls and women have ... we are emotional spenders. Yes, that's right! A girl's nature is to use her feelings when she is spending money. For example, a girl is more likely to spend her spare money on a pair of shoes than deposit the money in a savings account. Here's another example for you: A girl is more likely to lend her spare money to a friend or relative rather than save it for herself. In many cases, girls and women lose relationships because we loan something of value, like money, to friends or relatives and never get it back.

Think about these questions:

- Have you ever borrowed from or lent to a friend or relative? It could have been money, clothes, shoes, or anything important to you.
- Did you give back the borrowed item when you said you would?
- Did the friend or relative give you back the borrowed item like they agreed they would?
- If the item was returned late or not given back at all, how did it make you feel?
- If you returned the item late or not at all, did you feel ashamed?
- Were you embarrassed?
- Did you feel like your friend or relative would not trust you again and therefore you could not ask to borrow from them again?
- If you were the one who received your returned item late or not at all, did you get angry?

- Did you feel like you could not trust your friend or relative to do as they say?
- Did it make you feel like you would not lend to them again?

In a sense, these questions reflect what this book is all about ... character and trust. It illustrates how important your character or reputation is when you do the things you say you will do and how trust or assured reliance in you strengthens your character when you do as you say. Your character and having trust in your character determines your creditability. This means that character and trust determine whether or not you are worthy of belief or, in this case, whether or not you are worthy of credit from a lender.

A lender is someone who loans you something and you agree to return it later. Going forward, we will refer to a lender as someone who lends money. The term creditor will refer to those who lend money or services such as phone, utilities, and insurance. *My goal through this book is to inspire you to want to maintain a high degree of credit worthiness.*

Credit ABCs is a fun and easy-reading book that explains the elementary facts about credit. Credit is when something of value is lent to another person with the agreement that the other person will repay or return the borrowed item at a later date. When the other person returns the borrowed item as agreed, that person is demonstrating positive credit responsibility. The primary purpose of *Credit ABCs for Girls* is to raise awareness of credit responsibility for older teenage girls.

As a teenage girl soon to become 18 years old, you have a lot of responsibility waiting ahead. You will probably be entering college soon or going straight into the workforce. Either way, organizations and institutions will get your name and start contacting you because you will be of age for them to offer you credit. The organizations and institutions I speak of are called banks and credit card companies. Each year, many teenagers turn 18 years old and become eligible to establish credit. Some common reasons for establishing credit are cell phone

contracts, car loans, and even employment. In addition, later in life you will need credit to purchase a house. We will talk more about establishing credit in chapter 2.

Banks and credit card companies get very excited about 18-year-olds because they are a brand-new group of potential customers that are free of any negative credit history. This is good for banks and credit card companies because they make their money lending money to credit-worthy adults. However, they also make more money from their customers by charging fees when customers pay late or spend more than their credit limit allows ... this situation is good for the banks and credit card companies but bad for their customers!

My goal is to make sure you never become one of these unfortunate customers by inspiring you to always pay your bills on time. You will learn the importance of paying your bills on time in chapter 2.

Now go back to the series of questions I asked you earlier. When a lender lends you money and you fail to repay the lender when you agree to or fail to pay them back at all, instead of getting angry, the lender reports your name and payment behavior to credit-reporting agencies known as credit bureaus. When this happens, everyone knows you can't be trusted to repay your debt. Debt is the total amount you owe to the lender. You will learn more about credit bureaus in chapter 2.

When you wait too long to repay your debt or fail to repay your debt, your lender will send your name and payment behavior to a place called a collection agency. Chapter 3 is dedicated to understanding collection agencies.

Also, if you feel ashamed and embarrassed when you repay your debts late or don't repay them at all to friends and relatives, you will experience these same feelings when dealing with lending institutions, and they will not try to make you feel better. The lender will not care about your feelings; they will only care about getting you to pay your debt. However, maintaining good credit-worthiness makes you feel good about yourself, and as you get older, you will become very proud of yourself, not just because you pay your bills on time but also because you'll have access and privileges to so much more! In other words, the results of practicing positive credit responsibility can be a huge confidence builder.

This book is intended to be a launching pad for you to begin learning more about the huge world of credit. I encourage you to want to know more about credit and how it impacts your life. The references section at the end of the book provides web sites and mailing addresses of organizations that specialize in credit information you can learn from.

It is important for you to know that in today's society it is very hard to exist without credit. As a result, most adults will have credit. They will have excellent, good, fair, or poor credit, but they will have credit. People with excellent credit will be able to get anything they want and pay less for it, whereas people with poor credit are usually denied things unless they pay cash. People who are in between with good or fair credit can buy things, but they have to pay more for them because of higher interest rates. You will learn more about this in chapter 3. In addition, chapter 4 will teach you the basics about protecting your credit from those who take your credit without you knowing.

Another thing to know is that in our society, most people have to borrow money because they don't have large amounts of cash or they are saving their cash. So having excellent credit is very important to you. You can decide to have bad repayment behavior and live a life of hard financial times, or you can pay all your bills on time all the time and live life with confidence in knowing that you always have access to financial resources because of your excellent credit rating. For example, an advantage of paying your bills on time is that it demonstrates that you are responsible with credit, and as a result, you will be trusted with more money to buy nicer things. Thus, maintaining good credit worthiness and practicing positive credit responsibility can make a big difference in the rest of your life!

Please note: *Credit ABCs for Girls* will not discuss credit restoration, bankruptcy, interest rate programs, personal investments, stocks, or bank accounts. There are many other readings to address these subjects. However, *Credit ABCs for Girls* will inform, raise awareness, and set the foundation for positive credit responsibility for teenage girls approaching their eighteenth birthday.

Chapter 2

Credit ABCs: The Letter "A" About Credit Bureaus

"According to banks, a credit score is the quantitative measure of a person's character."

Credit Bureaus

Credit bureaus, also known as consumer reporting agencies (CRA), are where creditors report credit-payment history about a person who borrowed money or services from them. Also, business firms go to credit bureaus to get credit information on people who want to borrow money or services that require a credit check, such as cell phone contracts, renting apartments, and getting a car loan. To help you better understand, let's compare credit bureaus to something you're familiar with: high school.

Think of each creditor as a teacher. Just like your high school teacher records and reports all information about how well you do your assignments in class, creditors will do the same thing regarding how well you pay them back for money or services you borrow. They will record and report to the credit bureaus when you turn your payment in, if your payment is complete, and if your payment is on time.

There are three primary credit bureaus used by companies: Equifax, Experian, and TransUnion. For these bureaus, the most important piece of information about you is your social security number, also known as SSN. Your SSN is to you what an

ISBN is to a book. It is a nine-digit number that is unique to you. The first three digits give your area of location at birth. The second two digits are the group numbers, which identify your location more specifically within your area. The last four digits are serial numbers that have no specific meaning. They are assigned in order from 0001 to 9999, and when they are used up, the first five digits change. Just like high school, credit bureaus use your SSN to track and access your personal information. In addition, banks, hospitals, and businesses frequently use your SSN to reference personal information about you.

Credit Report

Another big thing that credit bureaus are very popular for is providing credit reports. Think of how your high school issues

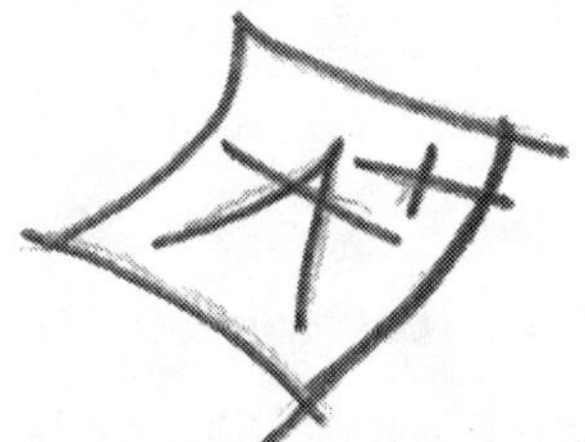

a report card for your academic grades. Well, a credit report is your financial-behavior report card to the world about your financial performance. A credit report, also called a consumer credit report, is a factual record of your credit activities. It reports all your credit accounts and outstanding loans, the balances on your credit cards and loans, and your bill-paying history. Lenders are allowed by credit-report laws to check your credit report and review it in order to determine whether or not to give you credit. In order to start to build a credit report, all you have to do is establish credit in the form of a credit card account, car loan, mortgage, or student loan. Most of the information on your credit report comes directly from the businesses you have accounts or outstanding loans with. When you pay your bills or fail to pay your bills, creditors usually report your credit information – good or bad – to credit bureaus.

For example, when you apply for college, the college will request a copy of your high school transcript. Your high school transcript gives the college administration a snapshot of your high school class and grade history. The same is true when applying for credit. When you apply for credit, the lending company will purchase your credit report from the credit bureau in order to get a snapshot of your credit activity; also known as payment history. Payment history addresses the following questions:

- How many loans do you have?
- How much were your loans?
- Did you pay the loan balance?
- Did you pay your monthly amount due on time?
- Did anyone place other negative information on your credit report such as a "judgment"?

A judgment is when a creditor reports your outstanding debt to the law by placing the amount you owe on your public records. This is usually the final step a creditor takes to collect your debt. *This is a very bad thing, and you never want this to happen to you!* Judgments are reported on your credit report and they stay on your credit report for a very long time after your debt is paid in full. Creditors are very hard on people who have judgments on their credit report, and in most cases, creditors will not loan money to you if you have a judgment.

In addition to businesses being able to purchase your credit report from credit bureaus, you are also entitled to purchase your own credit report from the credit bureaus. As a matter of fact, you are encouraged to get a copy of your credit report from each credit bureau to insure its accuracy. *A very important part of managing your credit requires you to review your credit report at least once a year.* Because this is so important, a credit report law was passed that will allow each individual to get one free copy of their credit report from each credit bureau each year. For more information, contact the Federal Trade Commission at www.ftc.gov or go to the Annual Credit Report website www.annualcreditreport.com. The Federal Trade Commission, also referred to as the FTC, is the government agency that enforces the credit laws that protect your right to get, use, and maintain credit.

For the most part, each credit bureau credit report is formatted differently, but there are four main categories of information on all credit reports as seen on page 19 in Figure 1: Example Credit Report:

1. Personal Information: Your credit report contains information that identifies you, including the following:

- Your name
- Your social security number
- Your current address and previous addresses
- Your phone number
- Your date of birth
- Your current employer and previous employers

2. Information Reported by the Lender: Your credit report includes your payment history with lenders such as:
   - Credit card companies
   - Car loans
   - House loans
3. Inquiries: Your credit report lists the lenders and credit grantors that have requested or received your credit report. Inquiries are important to lenders because they show how often you apply for credit. For example, if you were shopping for a car loan to purchase a car and allowed each car dealership to pull your credit report in order to check your credit score, the lender would consider you a high-risk customer; meaning that the lender would think you will probably pay your bills late and therefore the lender would charge you more interest dollars, which would result in you paying more than what the car is worth.

The lender would feel this way because you had to go many places in order to get the loan. Imagine paying too much money for something because you gave too many people permission to pull your credit report.

Here's a tip. When purchasing things that require you to get a loan, do your homework first: Know your credit score, know the interest rate you qualify for, know how much money you can afford to put down on the loan, and only let the lender you intend to get the loan from pull your credit report. When following this tip, a loan transaction will result in having only one inquiry on your credit report per credit purchase. This is how you manage inquiries and your credit score. Thus, the general rule is the fewer inquiries on your credit report, the better.

4. Public Records and Collection Agencies: Your credit report lists any items that may affect your credit, including:
    - Judgments
    - Bankruptcies
    - Collections

Let's see how credit reporting works ... We'll use "Blouses and Boots" department store as an example ...

- "Blouses and Boots" subscribes to the services of the three major credit bureaus: Equifax, Experian, and TransUnion.
- "Blouses and Boots" electronically reports to the credit bureaus on a monthly basis the payment

Example Credit Report

Personal Information

Jane Doe	322 Previous Address	Better Job	Good Job
203 My Address	Old Town, America 11111	Leader	Helper
Right Here, America 55555	Date of Birth: 1-30-1982	1999	1997
Phone: 555-555-5555	SSN# 222-22-2222		

Information Reported By Lender

LENDER NAME	DATE REPORTED	DATE OPENED	HIGH CREDIT	BALANCE	CURRENT RATING	HISTORICAL DELINQUENCY
Credit Card #1	4-07	6-97	$6,000	$1,500	Current	90 Day, 1998
Credit Card #2	4-07	9-97	$2,000	$1,900	Current	120+ Day, 1998
Car Loan	4-07	8-97	$20,000	$0	Current	
Mortgage	4-07	10-01	$130,000	$121,400	Current	

Inquiries

Authorized Inquiries

DATE	LENDER
3-31-07	Car Dealership
12-15-06	Clothing Store

Unauthorized Inquiries

DATE	LENDER
11-02-06	Cell Phone Company
2-08-07	Insurance Company

Public Records / Collection Agencies

2-98	Collection $500
5-98	Judgment $1,000 Satisfied 3-00

Figure 1

history of every customer who has an account with them.

- The credit bureaus keep a file on you and record in your file every month what “Blouses and Boots” reports to them.
- When an employer, lender, or insurer asks to see your credit file, the credit bureau generates a credit report.

The credit report assists employers, lenders, and insurers with the decision-making process. As seen in Figure 2: Credit Profile Lifecycle (CPL) shows how credit bureaus play a key role in your financial behavior. The CPL is when you establish credit with a creditor, the creditor reports your activity to the credit bureaus, and credit bureaus provide a credit report of your credit history to those who inquire, also known as credit history inquirers. So if you had three credit cards, a car loan, and so forth, each one would report your payment history to one or more credit bureaus. This information would be added to your file. Creditors report this information on a routine basis. Some creditors report monthly, quarterly, or annually.

Establishing Credit for the First Time

Now you may be asking yourself, how do I establish credit? Well, for a young lady just getting started, apply for a credit card issued by a retailer such as Sears, Macy’s, Texaco, etc., because retail and gas cards are much easier to get than a Visa® or MasterCard®. However, although gas cards are easy to get, don’t try to establish your credit history with only

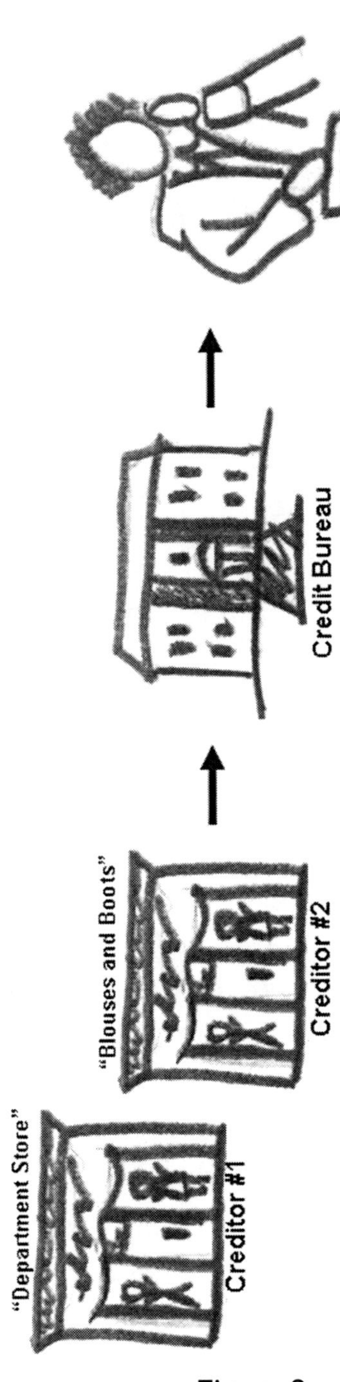
Credit Profile Lifecycle
"Department Store"
Creditor #1
"Blouses and Boots"
Creditor #2
• Reports to the credit bureau on a monthly basis the payment history of every customer who has an account with them
Credit Bureau
• Keeps a file and records in the file every month what a creditor reports to them about each credit customer
• When an employer or lender asks to see a person's credit file, the credit bureau generates a credit report
Credit History Inquirer
• Apartment Rental
• Insurance
• Bank Loan (Automobile, House, etc.)
• Phone Service
• Credit Card Application
• Employment Application
• Opening A Bank Account
• Utilities (Electric, Gas, Water)

Figure 2

a gas card (e.g., Texaco, Exxon, etc.) because these creditors rarely report credit histories to the credit bureaus unless you fail to pay your balance; however, you can use gas cards as a reference on a credit application. Also, you must be at least 18 years old to be approved for a credit card and you must have a job. However, in some instances, college students are not required to have a job.

Young ladies are often introduced to credit cards for the first time during their freshman year of college. A normal routine for credit card companies is to solicit new business from college campuses by offering students the opportunity to apply for a credit card usually with a small credit limit, something like $300. In order to get the students to apply, the credit card companies will offer free gifts like iPods and calling cards along with a low to zero interest rate. An interest rate is the fee a credit card company charges for the money used on the card. Interest is applied to monthly balances. For example, if you have a credit card balance of $150 and an interest rate of 19 percent, your interest charge for this month's bill will be $28.50. Therefore, your total credit card balance due is $178.50. Interest rates for credit cards average approximately 18 percent to 21 percent.

One of the biggest problems with this scenario is that the majority of young college girls don't know anything about credit responsibility, and in some cases, they don't know anything about credit at all. As a result, they apply and get approval for the credit card. Then, because they are not educated on how to

use and manage the credit card, the young ladies end up with poor credit. Consequently, these college girls grow up and spend several years trying to repair their credit. In the meantime, a large amount of money is spent through the years in high interest rates for purchases such as car loans, mortgages, insurance, etc. The *New York Times* once reported that when teenagers enroll in college they receive an average of 11 credit card solicitations a month and run up an average monthly debt of almost $3,000. *Wow, $3,000 a month ... that's a lot!* The research article attributed this outrageous debt to credit card companies enticing students with free gifts and teaser rates of 2.9 percent, which jump to 16.5 percent and soar to 24.5 percent as a penalty due to a few late payments. In many instances, the interest rate penalty increase will occur after you make one late payment. Teaser rates, also known as introductory rates, are usually very low interest rates, for example 1 percent, 2.9 percent, 4 percent, or in some cases 0 percent rates that increase after three months. An interest rate is important because it is the cost of borrowed money ... for example, the money you borrow from the credit card company when you use a credit card.

Credit Score

OK, let's go back to our high school comparison. Remember how we said the credit report is like your high school report card? Well, your high school report card assigns a grade of

A, B, C, D, or F for each class you take, and your grades are calculated into a GPA (grade point average) in order to measure your high school career performance. Just like the high school report card, the credit report is assigned a value similar to a GPA; it's called a credit score. A credit score is a measurement (excellent, good, fair, or poor) of a person's financial behavior and character. Just like a GPA tells if someone is a good student, a credit score is a three-digit number that helps lenders predict how likely a person is to repay her credit payments on time. The lender will ask: Will she pay and will

Excellent	Good	Fair	Poor
850 - 750	749 - 660	659 - 520	519 - 300

she pay on time? The credit score range is 300 - 850. The higher the credit score, the better your financial behavior! Of course, a poor credit score indicates that your credit is sick and is in need of credit repair. There are many books about credit restoration.

There is a secret formula used to calculate your credit score, and it is done by a company called FICO (Fair Isaac Corporation). So when you hear the term FICO score, know that it is referring to your credit score.

According to the Fair Isaac Corporation, your credit score is calculated based on the following:

- Your payment history — approximately 35 percent of your total credit score is based on this category. Late and missed payments can have huge negative impact on your credit score.

- How much you owe – approximately 30 percent of your total credit score is based on this category. Keep your credit card balances low because high balances can have a negative effect on your credit score. It is always best to keep your credit balance 50 percent below your total credit limit.
- Length of credit history – approximately 15 percent of your total credit score is based on this category. *In general, a longer credit history will increase your credit score.* When you are new to established credit, don't open a lot of new accounts too fast. New accounts will lower your average account age. This will have a larger affect on your credit score if you don't have a lot of other credit information such as mortgages or car loans. Rapid account buildup will make you look too risky to lenders.
- New credit – approximately 10 percent of your total credit score is based on this category. Several credit inquiries for the sake of opening new accounts will have a negative impact on your credit score.
- Types of credit in use – approximately 10 percent of your total credit score is based on this category. Your credit score will consider your mix of credit cards, retail accounts, installment loans, finance company accounts, and mortgage loans. (Note: Not all debt is bad debt – reasonable student loans and mortgages are considered "good" debt because these types of loans offer a positive return to the borrower. This is called an investment.)

As you can see, *paying your bills on time is very important because your payment history has the highest percentage weight!* Once you have been issued credit, it is very important that you are not late making payments or, even worse, miss making a monthly payment entirely. Missing a single payment will damage your credit score for years, and being late several times will come back to bite you! Be sure you don't damage your credit score needlessly – *always send your payment in at least 10 days before the due date to give plenty of time for your payment to be received.* The credit card companies report late and missed payments automatically to the credit bureaus by computer every month. If your payment hasn't been received by the due date shown on your statement, a negative entry may be placed on your credit report, and it isn't fun trying to get negative entries removed from your credit report. In addition to negative reporting on your credit report, late payments will cost you late fee charges out of your pocket! So don't adopt the attitude, "I'll pay that bill when I'm good and ready!" because you are only hurting yourself. Credit scores, if mismanaged, can fall fast, but it takes longer to improve … just like a GPA.

Another thing, income vs. expenses – don't spend more than you can pay off each month. Keep in mind that when you are issued your first retail credit card from Sears or whomever, you want to maintain an excellent credit rating so you can one day qualify for a Visa or MasterCard. Use your new credit card to buy small necessities, such as practical shoes and clothing, and pay your balance in full each month.

Paying off your balance each month or frequently shows you're a better credit risk. So when you're ready to apply for that Visa or MasterCard, your credit report will reflect that you paid off your credit card regularly. If you are unable to pay your balance in full, never have a credit balance greater than 50 percent of your credit limit. For example, if your credit card limit is $300, your total balance (the amount charged on your card) should not be more than $150. Also, never run your credit balance up to its limit! Once you have established a good payment history with a single trade account (e.g., Sears card, gas card), and you have sufficient income, you'll probably qualify for a standard credit card such as Visa and MasterCard.

Because the Equal Credit Opportunity Act (ECOA) protects you against discrimination, there are some things your FICO score will not use to calculate your score such as:

- Race, color, religion, national origin, sex, and marital status
- Age
- Salary, occupation, job title, date hired, or employment history
- Where you live (street, city, or state)

Let's talk more about interest rates for a moment. Interest rates are very important because they determine how much you pay for items when you borrow money. Not only do they apply to credit cards, but interest rates are also charged on car loans, student loans for college, and mortgages for a house as well as any other money you borrow. To see just how much impact interest rates have on what

you pay, consider this: Person A and Person B go to purchase a car. Person A has an excellent credit score and Person B has a fair credit score. They both purchase a car with a price tag of $20,000. Also, they both get financing (a loan) from the auto dealership for a term of four years. Because Person A has an excellent credit score, her interest rate is 4 percent. Because of Person B's fair credit score, her interest rate is 9 percent. As a result, Person A pays $25,188 (4 percent of $20,000 amortized over four years) for the car and Person B pays $31,961 (9 percent of $20,000 amortized over four years). Because Person A has a better credit score, she paid $6,773 less for the car. *This is how it is with all credit purchases. Practicing positive credit responsibility and maintaining an excellent to good credit score will lead to saving a lot of money!*

Obviously, paying your credit card bills is important to your credit score; however, paying other bills such as water, gas, and electric is just as important. Unlike credit card payments, these creditors do not report your monthly paying behavior to the credit bureaus when you pay on time, but they will report you when you miss payments. These creditors report you to collection agencies when you miss payments.

OK, now that you've learned how to establish credit, how credit bureaus create credit reports, and how credit reports are graded, chapter 3 will introduce you to collection agencies and the cost of bad credit.

QUIZ

Answer the following questions to measure your understanding of chapter 2.

1. There are four primary credit bureaus used by companies.

   a. True

   b. False

2. A credit bureau is also known as a:

   a. D&B

   b. CRA

   c. SSN

3. What is the most important information about you to a credit bureau?

   a. Name

   b. Income

   c. Social security number

4. Credit reports are provided by:

   a. Lenders

   b. Schools

   c. Credit bureaus

5. What does a credit report NOT reveal about you?
    a. Number of loans
    b. Income
    c. Amount of loans

6. How often should you review your credit report each year?
    a. Once
    b. Twice
    c. Never

7. What are the four sections of a credit report?
    a. Personal, Information Report by Lender, Inquiries, Public Records / Collections
    b. History, Information Report by Lender, Inquiries, Public Records / Collections
    c. Personal, Information Report by Lender, Inquiries, Employment

8. What are the components of the Credit Profile Lifecycle?
    a. Creditor, Credit Bureaus, Credit History Inquirers
    b. Collection Agency, Bank, Credit History Inquirers
    c. Department Store, Credit Bureaus, Banks

9. What is the purpose of a credit report?

a. To assist employers, lenders, and insurers with the decision-making process

b. To calculate the credit score

c. To get your personal information

10. What is an interest rate?

a. The cost of borrowing money

b. The amount you pay for sending your bill payment late

c. The amount you pay for going over your credit limit

11. A teaser rate is also known as an

a. Interest rate

b. Borrowing rate

c. Introductory rate

12. A credit score measures your

a. Credit limit

b. Financial behavior

c. High school performance

13. Credit scores are calculated by

a. FTC

b. FICO

c. ECOA

14. The greatest impact to your credit score calculation is

a. The length of your credit history

b. How much you owe

c. Your payment history

15. Always send your payment in at least five days before the due date.

a. True

b. False

16. When does an interest rate NOT apply?

a. Electric bill

b. Credit card

c. Student loan

Chapter 3

Credit ABCs: The Letter "B"
Bad Credit Equals Collection Agencies

"How many times would you ask someone to pay you back before you take action?"

- Have you ever borrowed something from someone ... money, clothes, books, anything ... and not given it back when you said you would?
- Did the person you borrowed from call you over and over and over again until you gave it back?
- If so, how did it make you feel?
- Did you get tired of them calling?
- Did you avoid their calls?
- Did you feel embarrassed?
- Did you feel pressured?

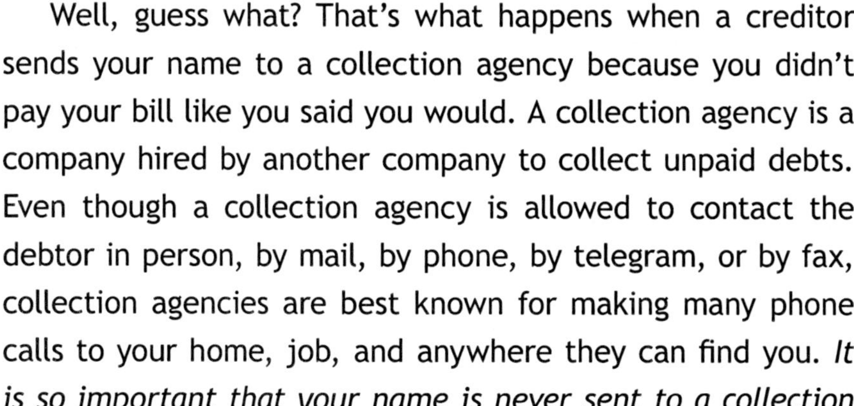

Well, guess what? That's what happens when a creditor sends your name to a collection agency because you didn't pay your bill like you said you would. A collection agency is a company hired by another company to collect unpaid debts. Even though a collection agency is allowed to contact the debtor in person, by mail, by phone, by telegram, or by fax, collection agencies are best known for making many phone calls to your home, job, and anywhere they can find you. *It is so important that your name is never sent to a collection agency! It is a nightmare that seems like it will never end!*

Everything about a collection agency is bad! When a creditor sends your account to the collection agency, your credit report will have negative information on it for at least seven years, your credit score goes down, and it costs you money. How does it cost you money? Because your credit score is lowered, lenders will require you to have higher interest rates, which could amount to thousands of dollars. Now imagine paying higher interest rates for at least seven years!

How Does It Work?

As stated in chapter 2, paying your bills and paying them on time is very important to demonstrating positive credit responsibility. Most bills such as credit cards, car loans, mortgages, and personal loans require you to pay an amount each month until the debt is paid in full. However, bills such as phone, cable, gas, and electric require you to pay a monthly amount until you stop using the service. When you make your payments on time each month, everybody is happy, and your credit rating is in good to excellent condition. However, making late payments or missing payments could land you on the collection agency list.

When you make a payment 30 days or more past the due date, the creditor will report this information to the credit bureaus as a late-payment status. In addition, they will continue to report it late until you pay the late balance amount in full, and they will include the number of days you are late in increments of 30 ... 30 days, 60 days, 90 days, and 120 days. After you are 30 days late, a creditor has the right to send your account to a collection agency. When this happens, the collection agency becomes your creditor and will

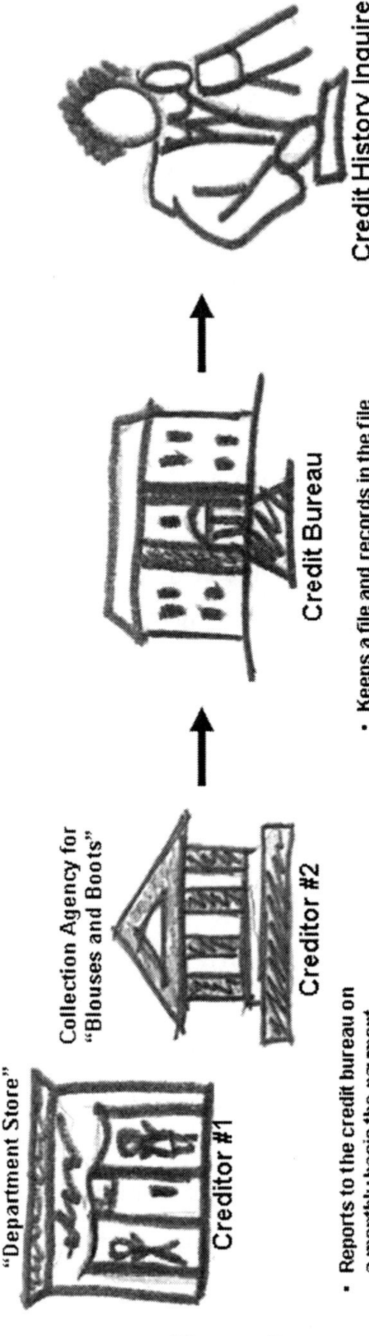
Credit Profile Lifecycle
(adjusted for collection agency)
“Department Store”
Creditor #1
Collection Agency for “Blouses and Boots”
Creditor #2
Credit Bureau
Credit History Inquirer
• Reports to the credit bureau on a monthly basis the payment history of every customer who has an account with them
• Keeps a file and records in the file every month what a creditor reports to them about each credit customer
• When an employer or lender asks to see a person's credit file, the credit bureau generates a credit report
• Apartment Rental
• Insurance
• Bank Loan (Automobile, House, etc.)
• Phone Service
• Credit Card Application
• Employment Application
• Opening A Bank Account
• Utilities (Electric, Gas, Water)

Figure 3

make several attempts to contact you in order to collect the balance due. In the meantime, the collection agency will start reporting your credit information to the credit bureaus for that specific account. Figure 3: adjusted Credit Profile Lifecycle illustrates this point.

Collection agencies fall into the "your payment history" category, and they represent negative reporting on your credit report. The collection account will appear on your credit report showing the name of the collection agency and the amount you owe. Also, in some cases the collection agency's contact information will be listed. Collection accounts remain on your credit report for a minimum of seven years. If you pay off your collection account before the end of seven years, the item will not be removed from your credit report. The status of the account will change to "paid."

Actually, it doesn't matter if you pay your late payment early or late; the most important message is NOT to pay your bills late at all so that you will not be reported to a collection agency!

How Does It Impact Your Credit Score?

As mentioned above, collection agencies are considered negative information reported on your credit report. You never want your account to be sent to a collection agency and then reported by the collection agency. When a creditor sees a collection agency on your credit report, it tells him that you can't be trusted to pay your bills on time or at all.

Because collection agencies fall into the "your payment history" category, the FICO score calculator will give a 35 percent weight factor to the negative collection agency information when calculating your credit score; meaning that *each collection account will drive your credit score way down. In addition, because the collection account stays on your credit report for at least seven years, your score will stay low for a long time, making it very hard to bring back up.*

How Much Does It Cost?

Collection accounts not only lower your credit score, but they also tell creditors that you are a big credit risk, and as a result, the creditors will charge you more money (interest) for the loan or service; that is, if the creditor chooses to lend to you. Sometimes, creditors will deny a credit request because it is too risky.

As stated in the previous chapter, interest is the cost of the loan. Every loan will have an interest charge. This is how lenders get paid for loaning you money. You must always remember that lending money is a business too, and businesses are in business to make money. *NOTHING is free!* On the other hand, service lenders (gas, electric, phone, and water) don't charge interest, but instead they charge you a service fee. Just like interest, a service fee is the cost to you for the service provider supplying the service. However, a primary difference between a service fee and an interest rate is that a service fee is not determined by your credit score.

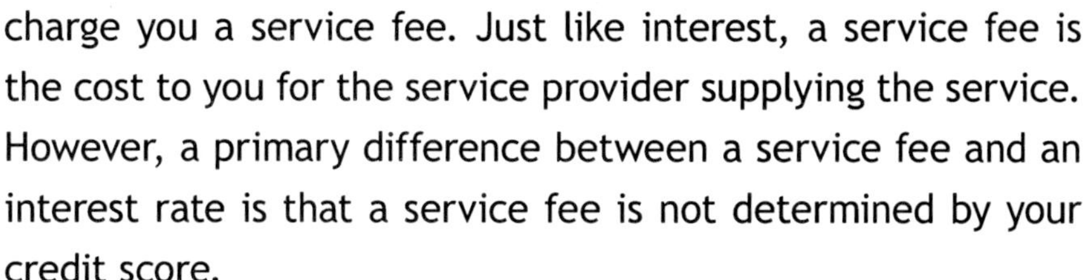

Here's what it's like when a person applies for credit, and there's already a collection agency on her credit report:

- A young lady fills out a credit application to apply for a clothing store credit card;
- When the clothing store processes the credit application, the clothing store requests a credit history from the credit bureau;
- The credit bureau sends the clothing store the young lady's credit report, which also includes her credit score;
- The clothing store sees her LOW credit score, which makes them look at the details of her credit report;
- On her credit report, the clothing store sees a collection agency listed as well as other things; and
- As a result, the clothing store issues the young lady a credit card, but she will have to pay 30 percent interest instead of 21 percent because of her low credit score and credit details.

In this scenario, because the young lady has a low credit score resulting from a collection account, she will have to pay hundreds more in interest.

Remember how we compared the credit score to a GPA

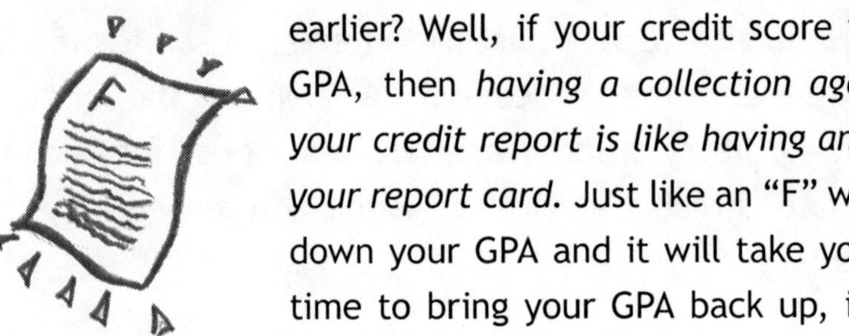

earlier? Well, if your credit score is like a GPA, then *having a collection agency on your credit report is like having an "F" on your report card.* Just like an "F" will bring down your GPA and it will take you much time to bring your GPA back up, it works the same when you have a collection agency on your credit report. Collection agencies bring down your credit score, and they stay on your report for seven years regardless of whether you pay your debt off early or not. *In other words, it will take at least seven years to bring your credit score back up.*

Overall, what you need to remember most about collection agencies is how not to get your account sent to an agency. You do this by paying your bills on time and in full. As shown on the next page, Figure 4: Accounts That Qualify for Collection Agencies gives you a point of reference for late payments that qualify for collection agencies.

Even though Figure 4 indicates that paying a bill 1-29 days late does not result in a report to the collection agency, enough late payments (especially those close to the 30-day mark) might result in a collections notice. So just don't take a chance and be responsible in paying your bills on time.

OK, now that you know how to keep collection agencies off your credit report, it's time to learn how to protect your credit from thieves. Chapter 4 will explore the importance of credit protection.

Accounts That Qualify for Collection Agencies

	Negative Impact on Credit Report	Lower Credit Score	Interest Applied	Late Fee	Sent to Collection Agency
1 – 29 Days Late	No. Not reported as late	No	Yes	Yes	No
30 Days Late	Yes. Reported as late	Yes	Yes	Yes	Probably not but creditor has the right to do so
60 Days Late	Yes. Reported as late	Yes	Yes	Yes	Probably not but creditor has the right to do so
90 Days Late	Yes. Reported as late	Yes	Yes	Yes	Most likely yes
120 Days Late	Yes. Reported as late	Yes	Yes	Yes	Most likely yes
Missed Payment (Stop Paying)	Yes. Reported as late	Yes	Yes	Yes	Yes

Figure 4

QUIZ

Answer the following questions to measure your understanding of chapter 3.

1. A collection agency is hired by companies to collect debt.
   a. True
   b. False

2. A collection agency on your credit report increases your credit score.
   a. True
   b. False

3. If you pay your bill 30 days late, can a company send your account to a collection agency?
   a. Yes
   b. No

4. How will a collection agency on your credit report be used in the calculation of your credit score?
   a. How much you owe
   b. The length of your credit history
   c. Your payment history

5. How long does a collection agency stay on your credit report?
   a. Three years
   b. Five years
   c. Seven years

6. How does a collection agency on your credit report cost you money?
   a. Higher monthly payments
   b. Increased interest rates
   c. Service fees

Chapter 4

Credit ABCs: The Letter "C"
Credit Protection

"Your credit is your most valuable personal asset. Guard it with your life." Marimeko Elie, bad-credit survivor

The "C" in *Credit ABCs*, credit protection, is very important to the measurement of your financial performance. Because you are young and just starting to build a credit history, you will begin your credit life in excellent condition, always paying your bills on time and paying your credit cards off. *As a result of your great credit, you are a number one target for identity theft.*

Why It Is Important

Identity theft is when someone uses your personal information without your permission for financial or another type of gain. In a lot of cases, the person who steals personal information is someone who is known to the victim. Often, teenage girls freely hand over their personal information to friends and family members. For example, teenage girls will give their credit card to a best girlfriend so that the friend can go and purchase shoes or pay a personal bill. Another example is that teenage girls will use their credit to open a phone account or utility account for their boyfriends or family

members. These are all examples of poor credit management and credit irresponsibility. These are ways to expose yourself and leave room for someone to use your credit without your permission.

In addition, people who are victims of Identity Theft can face many kinds of bad problems such as:

- Having their credit score destroyed, which would lead to high interest rates for loans and credit cards
- Receiving crazy calls from collection agencies for charges they didn't create
- Having money withdrawn unknowingly from their bank account
- Having problems opening a bank account
- Ending up with a mistaken criminal record and possibly going to jail

Ways to Protect

For these reasons, it is very important that you keep a close eye on your credit and protect it like you protect your life. It is very important that you be careful about leaving your personal information out for all to see as well as handing your credit information over to friends and family for them to freely use. *Here are a few things you can do to protect yourself from identity theft:*

- Protect your social security number. Don't give your SSN unless it is absolutely necessary. Don't carry it around in your purse, and shred all documents that have your SSN on them if you don't need them anymore.

- Be sure to protect your mail. Shred any mail that has account numbers or "pre-approved" credit offers on it.
- Shred all documents with any personal information on them before throwing them into garbage ... i.e., home address, bank account number, social security number, etc.
- Once you establish credit, contact one of the credit bureaus and purchase a credit-monitoring product so that you can be notified each time your credit changes. If you don't choose to purchase a monitoring product, you must at least order a free copy of your credit report once a year.

As mentioned in chapter 2, you should always get a free copy of your credit report each year. This will allow you to see if any unauthorized activity or incorrect information has been placed on your credit report. For example,

- There could be incorrect information on your report because you share the same name or have a similar SSN to someone else and the information somehow got mixed up.
- Your parents or other family members could have purchased something using your personal data when you were younger, causing it to be placed on your credit record.

Also, you can invest in a credit-monitoring tool from either of the credit bureaus. A credit-monitoring tool will alert you each time that there has been a change to the information on your credit report. I suggest you contact Equifax, Experian, or TransUnion for more information regarding the monitoring tool. Please see the reference section of this book for credit bureau contact information.

In order to protect your credit, just remember to always guard your personal information like a secret and never share it with anyone. Check your credit reports each year for accuracy, and consider investing in a credit-monitoring tool from one of the credit bureaus.

QUIZ

Answer the following questions to measure your understanding of chapter 4.

1. Can you become an identity theft victim by someone you know?
   a. Yes
   b. No

2. As a victim of identity theft, you can
   a. Have a lower credit score
   b. Go to jail
   c. Both a and b

3. How can you protect yourself from identity theft?
   a. Secure your social security number
   b. Protect your mail
   c. Both a and b

4. Is shredding all documents with your personal information on them a way to protect your credit?
   a. Yes
   b. No

5. Purchasing a credit-monitoring product will NOT help you protect your credit.
    a. True
    b. False

6. What could cause incorrect information to be placed on your credit report?
    a. You share the same name with someone else
    b. You have a similar social security number to someone else's
    c. Both a and b

Chapter 5

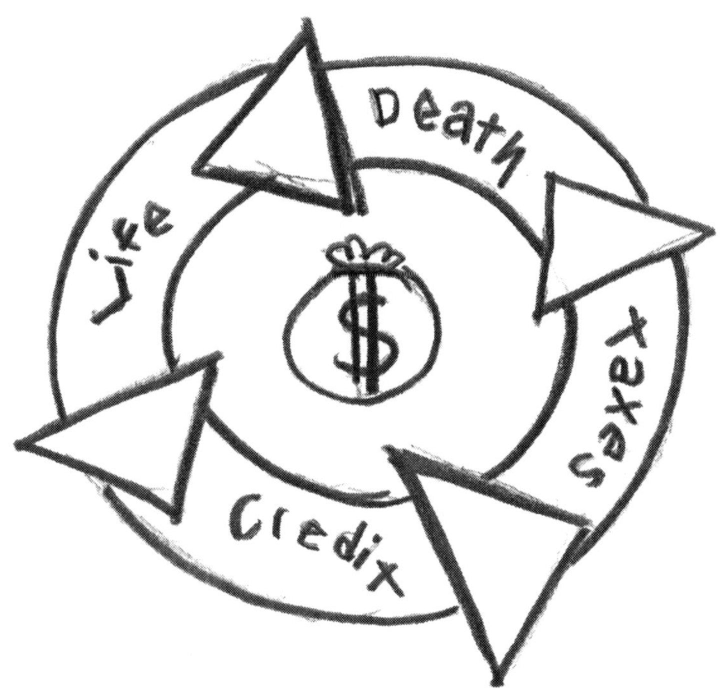

Credit ABCs Conclusion

"Never forget, there are four things that will never change: life, death, taxes, and credit. Also, don't forget, each one of these four things is a huge money-making industry that generates billions of dollars for our U.S. economy."

Congratulations! Now that you know your Credit ABCs, you will be equipped with simple but powerful knowledge that will have a huge positive impact on the rest of your life. *As you move forward into your adult life, you will begin to notice that so much of your life will be tied to your credit status.* For example, when you do any of the activities listed below, your credit will be checked in order to determine if you will be allowed to successfully participate in the activity and if so, how you should be charged to do so:

- Purchase a cell phone, car, or house
- Rent an apartment
- Apply for a credit card
- Subscribe to utility services such as gas or electric
- Apply for a job
- Open a bank account

- Apply for a bank loan
- Apply for insurance

It's clear that credit and the need for positive credit responsibility is just as much a permanent fixture in our society as being born into life, dying and moving on spiritually, and paying taxes to live in our country. In addition to the continuous existence of credit, it is important to mention that credit does not discriminate. All persons are eligible to establish credit:

- All nationalities
- All religions
- All genders
- All economic status
- All lifestyles
- Ages 18 and above

Properly managing your credit will lead to excellent financial behavior, and excellent financial behavior will guarantee big rewards! Some of these guaranteed rewards are listed below:

- Big SAVINGS from lower interest rates on credit cards, auto loans, house loans, and insurance policies. Let's compare good credit to a store sale that offers discounts. As long as you have good credit, you will always get a sale on life from discounts of lower interest rates.
- Easy access to things like apartments, cell phone contracts, bank accounts, loans, jobs, and credit cards. When a person has bad credit, it is common for them to be denied access or the right to have the items just

mentioned. In other words, bad credit takes away from your independence and ability to function with tools you need for everyday life!

You should know that you are at the threshold of something big, and you are about to walk into the next stage of your life: adulthood, becoming a woman. Good credit and knowing how to manage your finances properly is just as important as having a good education and job, because these are the things that establish the foundation blocks for your life.

Once you become 18 years old, a whole new group of people and institutions will start offering you things such as credit cards. They will make it look so easy, they will give you gifts, and they will tell you that it costs you nothing. But if you don't have enough knowledge to be responsible with your credit, it could cost you everything: your dreams, bigger opportunities, and, of course, money.

So, study your Credit ABCs, continue to learn more about credit as you grow, and demonstrate responsibility when managing your credit.

Also, as you learn more about credit and how it is managed, you might find that you have a career interest in the subject matter as well. Credit is a huge industry that contributes billions of dollars to the U.S. economy. For example, a Public Broadcasting System (PBS) Frontline special, "The History of Credit Cards," reported that the credit card industry alone was a whopping $30 billion industry in 2005. The credit industry is definitely growing, and it will always exist.

Quiz Answers

Chapter 2

1. b. False
2. b. CRA
3. c. Social security number
4. c. Credit bureaus
5. b. Income
6. a. Once
7. a. Personal, Information Report by Lender, Inquiries, Public Records / Collections
8. a. Creditor, Credit Bureaus, Credit History Inquirers
9. a. To assist employers, lenders, and insurers with the decision-making process
10. a. The cost of borrowing money

11. c. Introductory rate

12. b. Financial behavior

13. b. FICO

14. c. Your payment history

15. b. False

16. a. Electric bill

Chapter 3

1. a. True

2. b. False

3. a. Yes

4. c. Your payment history

5. c. Seven years

6. b. Increased interest rates

Chapter 4

1. a. Yes

2. c. Both a and b

3. c. Both a and b

4. a. Yes

5. b. False

6. c. Both a and b

Glossary of Terms

Collection Agency: A company hired by another company to collect unpaid debts.

Credit: When something of value is lent to another person with the agreement that the other person will repay or return the borrowed item at a later date.

Credit Bureaus: Where creditors report credit-payment history about a person who borrowed money or services from them. Also known as consumer reporting agencies (CRA)

Credit-Monitoring Tool: Alerts you each time there has been a change to the information on your credit report.

Credit Profile Lifecycle: The cycle that results from you establishing credit with a creditor, the creditor reporting your activity to the credit bureaus, and credit bureaus providing a credit report of your credit history to those who inquire.

Credit Report: A factual record of your credit activities. Also called a consumer credit report.

Credit Score: A measurement (poor, good, or excellent) of a person's financial health (trust and character). It is a three-digit number that helps creditors predict how likely a person is to repay her credit payments (obligations) on time. The credit score range is 300 - 850. The higher the credit score, the better your financial health will be viewed.

Creditor: Those who lend money or services such as phone, utilities, and insurance.

Debt: The total amount you owe the lender.

Financial credit: When money is lent to another person with the agreement that the other person will repay the money at a later date. Usually the money is repaid with interest.

Federal Trade Commission: The government agency that regulates the credit industry. Also referred to as the FTC.

FICO Score: Refers to your credit score calculated by a company called FICO (Fair Isaac Corporation).

Identity Theft: When someone uses your personal information without your permission for financial or other gain.

Interest rate: The fee that a lender charges for the use of borrowed money. For example, credit cards and bank loans.

Judgment: When a creditor reports your outstanding debt to the law by placing the amount you owe on your public records.

Lender: Someone who loans you something that you agree to return it later.

Payment History: A snapshot of your credit activity and behavior.

Positive Credit Responsibility: The demonstration of a person returning borrowed items as agreed.

References

Credit Bureaus:

- Equifax:
  www.equifax.com
  (404) 885-8000 – Corporate Headquarters

- Experian:
  www.experian.com
  (888) 397-3742

- TransUnion:
  www.transunion.com
  (800) 916-8800

Organizations:

- Fair Isaac Corporation: www.myfico.com

- Federal Trade Commission: www.ftc.gov/credit

Books:

- *Credit Bureaus: Dirty Little Secrets*, by Jason R. Rich

Printed in the United States
119520LV00002B/1-273/P

9 781434 365019